FIELD OF FLOWERS
A DIARY OF POEMS

Tedious and intricate
Sharp turns,
Loops and swirls
Under, over,
Crisis-cross,
Knit one, two purl

Designs are woven carefully,
In the fabric of life
They armor my garments,
Cast shadows,
From the glow of my inner light

I map my route on sequin paved ways,
My mind is all a haze,
I get lost in the stray-aways
Between the forests of frays,
Within the grey I fade

AS GOD KNITS MY QUILT

I

He— was my first smell of freedom; the first brush of sunlight on my raw, cold skin. He would be the first of many to teach me how to love a man. He was the template for the rest of my men to follow— including me.

Small flame,
Small ember
Small frame,
Big gestures
Shine bright,
Shine orange
Crackle loudly—
Warm warns
Move smooth,
Move slight
Move soft,
Move light
Like a moth
Singed wings
Burnt furs,
Burning queens
Boiled bodies,
Ego murders,
Falsities—

Men are torture

MEN

JULY 31, 2011

You're an enigma
You blow my mind
How sweet and divine
Flame throw slick rhymes
A beautiful touch,
Gorgeous features—
Lovely,
        Antique,
            Subtle

Focus with vigor,
I'm slain by your eyes
Impale the pavement,
Left tracks on my mind
You left your mark,
Found me in the dark
Your hand in mine,
Ignited the spark
Something different—
Deeper
        tones
Broad
        bones:

      Fully grown

Deep and wide:
His jawline
Big, white teeth,
For his lush lips to hide

You blow my mind,
But soothe me so

And pieced it back
You said
"Hello"

What do I say?
I want him to stay
My lips ajar,
Eyes filled with stars

I'm tongue tied and high,
How do I reply?
Reconnecting neurons,
Cut clean by his eyes

11

AUGUST 3, 2011

With a scream that can pierce the ears of Zeus...

Everything shatters—
Including me

I *break*;

       On the floor, I lay
             In pieces and shards,
                   Where the dust-mites play

This is what you've caused,
       You won't help me clean;
              Cuts from these sharp edges,

As he   me with a bandage
    taunts

AUGUST 5, 2011

The pound of a thousand drums,
Could not match the sound,
Of my heart's hum

               Yet—

I stand so still and calm,

               Inside,

I'm buzzing from cupid's stun gun

               Blood baptized currents,
               In my body,
               Pulsed through my heart—
               My lungs start to swell

               A powerful boom,
               That causes souls,
               To dance,
               And celebrate the miracle

Death is defeated another again,
With one note at a time
As we sing songs,
Of praise and promise,
With voices so
Sublime

Our unveiled eyes now
               Realize lies,
               Made by monsters that

Were disguised,

As lovers

Our voices ring to
Fill the voids,
How sweet the sound,
Of our harmonious noise

Fallen tears crash on the page,
Drops small and light,
Like autumn rain
They take the shape,
Of morning dew,
So rare and few

Love knows no bounds,
All range is reached;
Our song has yet,
To reach its peak

Our souls,
They sing with
Blended ring
I hear the music,
In all we do

From the mouths of babes,
Comes love's sweet sound,

As I write this note to you

AUGUST 9, 2011

In my eyes...

You can't look
You'll see yourself,
And what you took
You'll see the reason,
For all the tears
Brimming these eyes—
Water my fears

Because of you,
There's now a flood
Left me in the dust,
To cradle the mud

I'm too weak,
I can't speak;
I can't move
You don't sooth
You stand there to
Watch me drown,
From the inside out,
Without
       one
         sound

Emotion raw,
Only God knows
It's too much;
Too fragile to touch

As you brush my hand away
My leave,

I take—
Your face is blank

You won't see me,
You feel no need
Your heart won't bleed;
Your skin could freeze
Your eyes turned blind,
Your browns won't shine
You still
          can't
            look
Into my eyes

OCTOBER 26, 2011

Sick from all of the poisonous fumes,
I singed the remains of my feelings for you
Hatred embers in a hollow heart
Burn away this love,
To make a new start
Ash and soot fill vacant spaces
Burnt remains,
Of how I pictured our faces
Let the heat dry all of my tears,
Straight from my duct,
                    One by one,
                        Disappear

I'll take myself so far away,
I'll leave you and I,
In the spot where you lay
You give me so much,
Of what I can't take
I'm one with the fire,
As I crackle and break

MAY 3, 2012

Copy and paste,
    Copy and paste,
        Copy and paste,

            Copy

Copies of you everywhere,
Pasted all over the place
The thought of you is enough
I can't escape what's in my face
The scorpion sting hurts too much,
Where is somewhere that I can feel safe?
A place for me, myself and I,
So I can let my soul revive
I need a supernatural place
I need metaphysical space
To quiet the mind,
Muffle the heart,
God take me there,
And
   leave
      no
       trace
I'm holding on to a hope so brave,
That seems to fade day by day
Stunned by your venom,
I want your embrace
To dream of a day when
I won't crave the taste
One day I'll acquire,
What I desire;
One day you won't be,
What I desire

OCTOBER 13, 2013

The smell of Bounce,
Makes me think of you

     When I put on cocoa butter,
     You're on my mind, too

When my breath smells a certain way
When I put the glassware away

Whenever I see,
Pine green chairs,
     At times,
     It's more than
     I can bear

       Do you even care?

I hear shards of your voice,
When I talk to your cousin

     Eggs make me think of you,
     When I buy myself a dozen

I think of you,
When I see the 14th floor
City bus doors unfold,
And I mourn

       I think of you

When I don't want to
Of you and your smells
Reinvented ice cubes

I think you

Often.

Nothing here is getting solved,
Ignorance is far from bliss

Validate my every thought,
I don't trust myself for shit

Pro reject from old prospects,
Lent me my emotional debts

Old receipts are all that's left,
I can't read them
They're all wet

Am I weak?
Am I too free?

Want too much?
Too many needs?

Is it greed?
I can't see—

Filled to the brim,
With visions of him

I can't seem to find the words,
So much here I can't convey

Thoughts I think sound so absurd,
Why'd I give myself away?

Often cloud my mind with others
I can't think; I feel so smothered

Why's my mind preoccupied,
With thoughts and feelings,

That aren't mine?

My life would be so sublime,
Headspace for important things

Reclaim space I'm renting out,
Really see what life's about

Choosing to give up my space
Giving parts of me away

I can't seem to shut me off,
My brain is fogged,
I feel lost

Alone in my bones,
My issues are mine

Hulked and teary eyed,

Bottled up with pride

Can we trade our minds?
Yours seems more in line

Young,
In distress

I wouldn't have it any less,

Cliché

CLICHÉ

II

II

He traded his sweet, ripe fruit for my bitter bites.

To center myself,
To bring together
My scattered parts,
Pieces and severs
North, south
East and west
Do I not know?
Or did I forget?
Where did I put it?
Where did it go?
What am I looking for?
An ally or foe?

Hide and seek,
With my ego and me
It's never too far—
Crawling under scars
Battle wounds,
Made by harpoons
By oppressive tongues,
They impale my lungs
Under earth's crust,
I look for my worth
Does he know my worth?
Crawl so deep it hurts

Swimming the seas,
Of emotion and pride,
I search wide,
And sink deep to dive
Nothing but fear
That caused these tears
They made this dark sea,
In canyons carved deep

Cross desert terrain,

Of hollow tubed veins
I bled love for years,
I've nothing left to give
My heart was meant for one,
But he took my life pump

Lifeless twigs collect,
This body's all that's left,
A bag to carry broken things,
To echo songs my heart would sing

Beyond my brown hide
Behind my brown eyes
Behind bones so dried
Inside my lush mind
Dangerous, wild lands,
Jungles in hot sands
Space scraped tree tops,
Roots deep,
Land locked
My thoughts and ideas,
Move quickly like Cheetahs
Bite sharp like White Tigers,
Weave webs like Bird Spiders

I peel back the thoughts,
Fight through the foliage
To locate myself,
To find who I was again
In my deep folds,
Through my webbed trees,
Under lit skies,
Is where I like to hide

WHERE AM I?

JUNE 28, 2012

I look at you,
      Not looking at me
A gorgeous moment—
      How bittersweet
What seems like seconds,
Of a carnal glance,
      Feels like a lifetime,
      Of a supernatural dance
Distracted with choices,
For light or dark roast

      I watch as you search,
      For the change in your pants

            I like the subtle moments,
            That happen when we're together
            Inconspicuous love affairs,
            With souls,
            No one could sever
            We dance for ages in spirit realms,
            Songs born from pure emotion
            To sounds of heart strings tugged,
            Between the fingers of God's angels
            We waltz across the clouds so free,
            Wind moves to mimic us
            Gliding through worlds of hymns and psalms,
            This moment with you is precious

I looked at you...
      You're not looking at me
Soon you will be and
I'll turn away quickly
I'll look up and smile,

And pretend I didn't see
Then you'll sit next to me,
After ordering iced coffee

JULY 28, 2012

Gorgeous light crowns his face
Privileged to have him at my side

Sharing in the glory,
Of his presence with others

I bask in his sun,
Enjoying what's mine

To carry on,
With my selfish stance;
Barriers protect,
To ward off the lonely

A scarecrow made,
With my own two hands

But the truth is that
I scare so easily

Faith + work yields creation,
And the climb will take us high

But we stand still on a plateau,
As we watch our bloomed love die

My gargoyles are weathered,
My scarecrow is limp

His boredom is no secret:
He won't let me touch him

His nose burns my ears,

My tears stain my face

Nervous to try again—
He'll put me in my place

His light feels nice,
But his light has a price
Truth is what's mine:
Where his light likes to shine

Out of the dark,
And in my face
          Until this point,
          I made me blind

In my mind,
He can't see them:
The things I've done,
To me,
And mine

All the ways boys had their way,
Curious vultures out to play

Deliverance is mine,
From the hurt and the lies

One more drop of strength,
To pry my mind's eye

Fingers to knuckles,
Our hands are locked

He writes his name,
Upon my heart

I try to write my name on his;
My ink won't show on his brown skin

Immune to me and what I bring

Back on my bullshit

I can't chance it

I can't let him go

Won't let his eyes wander
They seem so much better,
When I'm so lackluster

SEPTEMBER 2, 2012

My stomach trembles in fear,
Because of what he might say
Angry butterflies sting
       And stab,
Where they lay
Violently attacking,
All good feels I had left
Afraid of what might pass,
Through the seam of his lips

Flashbacks and flash floods,
Of words used in dismay
Things I'ven't felt,
Since last Valentine's Day

This is a cruel feeling,
This,
Is reality
Is this a farce,
Or how it's meant to be?

I struggle to keep composure;
To keep the tears within the brim
My eyes make rain,
With every fleeting thought of him
Here unraveling before my being,
Is a union fresh and new
Everything I thought was present,
Was fading out of view

I took our lives into my hands,
And told him how he was my man
All this thinking,

Trying to plan
On ways to say,
We're *more* than friends

What's there left to lose?
What's here left to rot?
If I'm not *his* man,
At least I've done my lot
Cause he's all I've got,
I'd say that's a lot—

      Yet,

My fess up this eve,
Earned the key to his heart

SEPTEMBER 8, 2012

Non-verbals say no,
By the one who won't let me go
Face to face; my nose with his
But in our eyes,
One side blind

Slumber sounds through nostrils so flared,
My lungs deflate; he steals my air
Heavy sounds from my gentle giant
I try not to move though his snore shakes the trees
My love for him could move the tallest mountain;
One heartbeat could move planets with ease

I know he's fine without what I bring,
Each breath tells the truth that lies deep within
By the end of tonight,
If I know nothing else,
I at least know that I,
Indeed,
Love him

And so I stay with these words locked away
Wrapped in his arms encased in ebony charm
At rest on his chest; this isn't easy to say
When I move he tugs; his actions plainly convey that
Even asleep,
He feels my love move away
Submission from me lets him know it's okay
He wants me close; he wants me near
He wants me to know that I'm needed
Right here

With one final pull and one last tug,

The lax of his embrace becomes a soft hug
I stop the fight and he raises me high
So I might hear as his mouth marries my ear...

He's sorry

SEPTEMBER 26, 2012

We all have our crosses to bear,
But is what you're doing really fair?
You expect as little from me as
Those of less nobility
Faulted for ignorance,
Of what tainted your spirit
This rough climb to glory—

Elite members of remembrance

It seems like you don't care,
What your outcome is
I wish I knew,
What the outcome is...

In your eyes I change faces,
Flashbacks of people who have cases
Files on deck of faulty, bounced checks
Overdrawn accounts and unpaid debts
I thought you were balanced,
You seemed so stable
I'm just now feeling,
The wobble in your table

What are you feeling?
You won't hold my hand
Where do we stand?
You're lost in foreign lands of
"buts" and "what ifs"
I'm trying to show you me,
It's you I'm trying to uplift
You make it hard for me to feel free

I want to love you here, right now
Locked in a cage with all that you need
Your mind's left behind with bad potentials
A toxic place for your soul to feed

I'm trying to make me yours,
But are you even mine?
      Am I that naive?
            Has love made me that blind?

Is this the sign to leave?
The grand goodbye,
Laid thick with subtlety
Fed my cue from platonic channels
I still give you more than I can handle

In my hands I hold with grace,
Your precious gift laid at my feet
You gave me your heart,
I wrapped it with lace
The force in your serve,
Admitted defeat
Around the barb,
And through the wire,
The lace is laid—
It lights you on fire

Is this too much,
Am I too little?
I don't deserve,
This meal that you serve
I've kept you blameless,
Baptized by my eyes
Omitting any part,
Is still seen as a lie...

I can't serve you well,
When you've got secrets to tell

Confess your sins and
Set yourself free,
Let me be for you,
What I'm supposed to be

AUGUST 15, 2014

With emotions bold,
So brazen how they finesse
What I feel right now says more,
Than what my words could ever express
Deep carves from bloody erosion
Scooped step stools,
That lead out of commotion
Romance and knife fights with
You cut me to bite size
Pieces of torn hide—
It's so easy for your knife,
      To glide,
           On my skin

I drown in my red sea,
Wondering if you'll ever see,
Crimson flowing west to east
North and south,
Gargled from my mouth
Currents strong,
Break through weak bones,
They,
Tore through my home
I'm,
Left me here to roam

You don't let me stop;
Just watched me go
Your tough love helped,
When energy got low
The climb isn't easy,
When there's blood,

To slip the grip
But when I'm done,
And I stand alone,
The first few steps,
I'm sure I'll trip

I'll learn to walk—
Just me and I

No lack of love,
No crippling cry

Before I was his,
Damn right I was mine

Continuously

'Til the day I die

AUGUST 15, 2014

Dodging the relapse like it's gym time
Post break up limbo; a different kind of FaceTime
You can do all you can to avoid the pummel,
Red rubber bullets will return you to the soil
Across half court he stands with the ball,
The only support I have left are my walls

I become predictable,
He moves with me,
There's no escape—
I'm shot in the face
My aura is bruised from the beating endured,
Is there any way to get a heart insured?
I crawled through the dust:
This emotional trench
To find my way to the safe, cold bench
I might be out because I got hit,
But this game isn't over,
I won't let myself quit

    Get over him

AUGUST 20, 2015

To conjure up the feelings of love at will,
Remind me,
Even now,
I love you still
To close my eyes and see you there,
To hear your voice fill my mental air
I pant at your gaze and feel your embrace
My mouth waters with the thought of your kiss...

Why do I do this?

I travel to a time and space,
Where our love never took a break
I go where my heart wanders,
And in your arms I find myself
Clung
To your brown slender body

But is that really your brown slender body?

What if memory serves me wrong and
I don't remember you at all
What if all I know is a lie and
There was no flame in your eyes,
When I last saw you

Come close,
With me...
The one who loved you most

I'm a bitter old queen with unsatisfied needs,
I tried growing some flowers but all I got were weeds
My love was too free,
I was too selfless for fees,
But now all I have,
Are bruised,
banged up
knees
I now trust no man,
Though some ask for my hand,
But they're too late,
Nigga leave or wait
For the day when maybe I can

PROBATION

III

III

Alive and well, I've had time to bloom. I've been through enough to recognize the beauty of a lotus hiding beneath the mud: I saw the beauty in him.

Sink right through,
Pierce the sky like a star
Robe yourself in darkness,
Remember who you are
Night is the time when visions arise
I wait for the sky to close its eyes
Black is the sheet that covers my deeds
Only while blind can I meet all my needs
I dance in the soil that covers my eyes
My steps,
Like fire,
Burn the sand of time
Trails of glass footprints show the moon is aglow
Conversations send messages from above to below
Night is the time for the Self to arrive
Night is the time for the dead to be alive
Here is when closed eyes trump those open wide
Between these threads of skin is where all my truth hides
Pick all the stars,
Pocket each one
Play with your imagination—
Moonchild, have fun
Speak your tongues and raise your voice
Say your thoughts,
Let spirit make choices
Take off your skin and finally feel the wind
Claim love and feel drunk without the spike of gin
Float on thin air and grin until it hurts
Because night time is the right time;
With darkness you knew love first
Wrap yourself in Black and remember who you are
For on this night you see yourself as the morning and evening
star

MOONCHILD

APRIL 12, 2015

I feel the warm sun and the cool breeze hit my body with such gentle force. At the same time, I feel your hand land on my leg and for a while both experiences felt one and the same. When your head found its way to my shoulder, your curls graze my face with a tickle and my heart flutters in reaction to it. The hairs on your head eclipse my sight and break the blue-orange sky into pieces; I saw the word "love" spelled through the coils into the sky. In these moments are when my emotions hiccup from the pressure of repression—they fight to shine through, bright like the sun on our faces. Just as strong as the waves roll from the Detroit shore to the Canadian coast, my feelings do the same throughout my body; everything at once and at once I am at peace.

You are my peace.

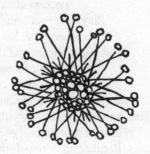

APRIL 22, 2015

Your curls make me dizzy and your laugh makes me flinch as jolts of electricity are passing through every receptor in my body. Not once has a message been translated as anything less than joyous. You're as gracious as a newborn and have a heart just as pure. I consider every chance, every opportunity to touch you a privilege that I hope you never think I take for granted.

To sleep next to you is to have the soundest sleep I've ever had. And some nights, when you're here, I can barely sleep a wink— your presence demands my attention and I gladly give it to you whenever lucid enough to direct it so.

I try to be sly with my glances onto your beautifully sculpted face; into the depths of your eyes I drown when they meet. It is your kiss alone that causes the planets to align. It is your kiss, dear Gage, that pulls my heart into your orbit. When you're near, my heart belongs to you and only you. It is only when it's in your hands that my blood can travel the canals in my body without it. When my heart is in your possession, I can never die. Come now, help me live forever. Claim my heart and hold it in your hands. You turn me immortal and grant me the pleasure of staying alive in your love. Be my savior and deliver me from the hands of death and every day I will remind you why you chose me in the first place.

APRIL 23, 2015

In this space,
It's hard to replace,
The feel of you being near
The scent behind your ear

It carries

Throughout this space,
The frame of your face
It haunts this place
This place,
   My place,
    My space,

     Outer space

MAY 5, 2015

Here

In this space where

Old miracles used to take place

Where

There was often

      One mind
Dressed
      With two faces

With one knee bent I would bow at your feet to

Give thanks for the honor of holding onto you

In this space,
      In these spaces

Pockets of magick glow

In the night of our minds,
           Hearts and
                Spirits

So that in the night of this room,
I could find you

Because you glow as

I do the same for you

I lay here alone with my heart and mind aglow with

No one to use me as a lantern

To find their way back to this sacred space

I am forced to realize that

My light is only attractive for so long
Before
The brightness blinds you and

I'm no longer visible

Change is uncomfortable
Tell me when it's over
I'll be too busy,
Not being sober
Pass the weed,
Drinks,
And turn on all the music
Drown out all construction noise,
I long to not be lucid

Growth is inevitable;
Coping's a full time job
I'm always in a constant state,
Of drowning in a song

The run was fun,
The jumps were high,
And friends were always new
But as this growth began to start,
I bid so many adieu

"Pull the weeds and keep the flowers"

So that leaves only few
But that's alright, because who's left,
Has proven to be true

As growth ensues,
And change is made,
I feel so many things
I'm always looking at my hand,
Imagining a ring
I think of life and how I'll start;
Who'll see me til the end?
How do I want to live my days,
With one or several men?

Several were fun,
But surely there's one,
Who'll make me love again

I deconstruct thoughts of the past,
Refurbished all software
It's made me think more critically
Even more self-aware
Now I sit in solitude,
Reviewing all these things
Through lenses blurred,
Words slurred,
From gin,
Grimes,
And greens

Change is inevitable,
Growth hurts like the truth
It's wonderful my disposition,
Is to welcome all things new
But that don't mean I want to feel,
Jack hammers and dumpster trucks
I'll take the finished product,
Until then,
I give no fucks

HELLO, MID TWENTIES

VI

IV

Yearning for him felt narcissistic

The way it feels to remember...
You
Everything I felt was true
More than I wanted to
Isn't that what you came for?
Didn't you want love?
Save it all for someone else
Another trophy on the shelf
A lesion on my mental health
I'm crazy
Drunk
Have I not,
Been here before?
My heart is still sore,
From the last man who took more
But what he took was given by me;
He can't take what I don't support

I had a hand in my heartache—

Torturous tuition for wisdom

Was it worth it?
Were we worth it?
Artistic babymomma
We created things together
You planted seeds unbeknownst—
The art I birthed in your name
But to you was it all a game
Bullet holes in a picture frame
Inside-out I'm turned again,
Cocooned

Evolved a better man
Isn't that the point, Peter Pan?

METHOD TO THE MADNESS

JULY 28, 2015

One of the more intimate exchanges to be had in a long time and in such a space: your space. You allowed me into your space and I can't, won't take that lightly. The light flickered, but the room was brighter than the sun. We were vulnerable and primal; we were organic. Unplanned in our minds but the stars were aligned in the sky to tell the tale of you and I together in that garage, with the old Ford, and the flickering fluorescent.

AUGUST 26, 2015

I lay here and
Wonder if
You'll become another souvenir
Steel bullets shot
To me from love like
Cannons
Holes that leak life onto pages of
Books and electronic forums
Shattered breast bones—
Ripped open chests
That have felt the touch of hands so soft

Then,
So rough

Each shell,
Carved with *his* initials
With me,
I carry to my bed to heal
I sew my wounds and
Examine the steel

Will you join the ranks of
Men who aim and fire?
Or will you break their mold,
And be my heart's desire?
Your need for space comes first at this time
I can't shake the idea,
Of one day you being mine

So I'll wait,
To see what time will bring...

Hopefully my muscle doesn't resemble a target ring this time

Unless the police want to join the fun
Between Cupid and men,
I get shot enough

OCTOBER 12, 2015

Art fills the spirit and has yet to be stabbed out

Tickling the skin,
But,
Never piercing the epidermis of its chambers
Our conversations have yet to
Make our bodies bleed anything

With skin translucent and nails sharp,
We scratch the surface of a
Potential masterpiece
Behind the hide of you and I,
Is love to share for eons at a time
            Who knows if it is meant for a lifetime?

Why preoccupy the mind with
Such morbid thoughts?

Feel the mysteries being drawn out
I feel yours resisting to show;
To be made known

I want to hold you,
            Caress your face,
                        Kiss your lips and
                                    Hold your hand

You have my heart right here,
Right now
And
When time pushes me forward,
Know this to be true
Right here and right now,

My heart belongs to you

OCTOBER 16, 2015

How high can the mountain top reach?
     How deep can the rabbit hole go?
How wide can the ocean shores separate?
     How fast can my heartbeat begin to race?

How bright can my soul glow from the sound of your
name?
How wide can my smile get from one look at your face?
     How sweet can the smell of your skin be to me?
     How long before these wants turn into needs?

How long before these feelings begin to erupt?
     How much will I feel before it becomes too
     much?
How heavy will I get before I'm light enough to soar?
     How long 'til I can employ the love I have in
     store?

Is there an end,
To the questions I have?
     All the variables to solve for,
     Using such intricate math
A different formula for all,
A new theorem for each one
     How long before I solve them all?
              I've only just begun

OCTOBER 25, 2015

Secrets come out at 4am
You smoke your poison,
And say you still love him
Staying awake trying to catch the info
Wondering what am I going do with this info
      Is he really vomiting all of this toward me
      though?

I'm grasping where he is,
I imagine the shitty space
      He's always traveling back in time
      I now know,
            He'll never be (fully) mine
His chapter's unfinished,
Unsure of full closure
The thought of one day,
Loving him again

Celestial warnings fill my belly

    ...

Or maybe just paranoia

Baited by flames to
Scorch these butterflies
Whose wings fan the fires
Lighting paths ahead:

Him and me
Me and him
Us and we
Him and he
Me and...me

NOVEMBER 13, 2015

I want more and
        You want him
Is there any one of us who'll win?
            You're wondering if you're still a sin?
                    Waiting for him to just say
                    when?
To leave me here,
To breathe his air

I'm jealous of a man that's not even (t)here

Our dialogue's a three way:
Me, you, and him always
Even while he's far away
Our conversations are on replay

I want more
I want the rest
Not just the remanence,
He left in your chest

I want your heart,
I want your love
You gave me a problem,
Impossible to solve

I want something,
Specific to us

Something,
That no one else can touch

Our auras intertwine,
Why can't you see?
You belong to him,
You allow yourself to be

  How long will it take,
Before you can belong to me?

APRIL 16, 2016

I see the signs,
> I know the patterns;
>> I know what comes before and after
I long for the feeling,
> Yet dread the adieux
For around every corner,
> There'll be another you

I've known this feeling
> I've felt it before
It's a matter of time,
Ere you slam the door

> You'll swoon and
> Slick your way inside
> Just when the grip gets loosed,
> You'll try to
> Kill me slow
> You'll,
> Say you didn't know
> You'll wring my heart out
> Clean and dry
> Lay lifeless on the floor
> You'll drain my scarlet bosom,
> All red cell you can get and
> When I think it's over,
> You won't let me forget,
> That it's you...

My dream come true

You'll dig your way inside my head,
And leave me black and blue
Down to a level so low,

I'm staring at your shoe
As I drown in that crimson,
From the steel that you shoot
I'll lie to myself and
Say it's just fine
And it's true

I'm just fine.

I'll beat myself even after death,
Because I was so blind
So blind that while this happens to me,
I think you're the perfect guy
So blind,
That as I'm lying there,
I think I'm up right
So blind that when this happens to me,
Your shoes become your eyes
I'll stare as if I'm gazing at you,
And smile because it's grand
I'll feel like I'm high on cloud nine,
But really I'm just dead
A zombie wanting more of
How you made me feel this way
A masochist for how it feels,
To be a human cave

You see inside,
Behind the hide,
And bones you tore apart
Is missing something deeply vital:
What's missing is my heart

I see the signs,
I know the patterns
I want so much to feel that I matter
Gasping so much as I spit and spatter

Up to my nose in blood from the cave,
Where drums,
Could not have beaten,
Any faster

JUNE 27, 2016

Fight or flight only does so much
In the grey the reaction goes both ways

Do I run or fight for the touch?
I ask if it will tickle or will it punch

I steal sweeps from your shirt,
A brush from your hands
Your arm swings close to me
Dramatic come and goes of your energy

Fair and unafraid you gift me your time
You might have resolved your feelings,
Unlike I've done with mine
Your eyes are,
So sublime...
With cheekbones high and
A smile that's kind

Oh gentle ox,
Pierce me softly
Must I say olé
To give the green light

SEPTEMBER 30, 2016

When did the spell begin?
     Where did I dive in?
         Who drew who in?

I need a sip of gin

Carnal notes from an angelic mouth
     Cries amped from the thrust of Pink Pussies
Because I thought that I missed out
     All these tears could fix any drought
What I do is of Satan and what you do is divine
     Am I supposed to pretend that everything is
     fine?

We aren't normal

I don't wish to see you the way I did

APRIL 4, 2017

I notice everything you do to
Make new ways to think about you
Seconds of footage make the memory for me,
Those seconds of you last me eternities

Morris code on the cymbals
       Ironing khakis on the carpet
Zebras on your magic farm
       Off-white girl on the black market

Walking on the balls of our feet
The face you made when I first heard you sing

Rumors of a steam room,
With red lights to taunt you

Some days I think of all of them...
Most days only a few

You're so silly

JUNE 29, 2017

A blast from the past like last week's fad,
Here comes the boyfriend that I never had

Here is the man who
Switched up the plan
I'm homegrown to love you;
Now you don't like men

I had here in my pocket,
Your heart,
Unshattered
But you held me at gunpoint,
Then asked me
"What's the matter?"

The work I put in
The time I entrust
The knife that *he* used to
Tear out all my guts
The songs that we shared and
Light that we'd beam
The love you said you'd
Blooming deep in you for me
The art
we created;
Our
spirits danced
for days
The laughter that we
shared and
Memories we made

I can't be angry,
Though I'm trying to be honest

There's no account to hold you to—
No deposit of a promise

APRIL 22, 2018

F

Longing for a memory of you
   But is my memory of you really true?
I reached out,
Looking for clues to
See if that you was
Really you
All the things you said
Were true,
'Cause what you said
Made me undo
If what was shared was all forgotten
   Does my name in your mouth feel rotten?
     Is it sour?
     Does it burn?
When you think of my face,
   Do you yearn?
Does the sound of my voice,
   Make you churn?
Do my parting gifts to you,
   Feel earned?
Do you think of the lessons,
   All the things that we learned?
Are your feelings for me,
   That hard to discern?

R

There's a feeling that's missing
There's a case overturned
I think of you daily

Like a judge,
You've adjured:

Me
We
Us

All of the above
We gave so much together
Most importantly: love
I gave myself so freely
You fit flush like a glove
Blowing each other's horns
Always begging for more

I played myself and
You played you too
We played and danced
That's the adult thing to do
We told the truth
No lies between us two
Shooting each other
Knowing
We're not bulletproof

A

There was a time when
I couldn't dream;
My dream was shining
Right in front of me
Live: in living color like
The meadows,
Skies, and
Seas
Now all I have to show for it,

Are bruised and banged up knees
You gave me so much shit
Put all of your stress on me
Unsure of who you are—
How you're growing into being
Which part of you you'll serve
Your Bible gives the cure
Your soul drinks this word
No; I don't think that's absurd
You had dreams to start again,
Fireproof armor
Perversion plans
Trying your best,
You said deep from your chest
Ripped from your diaphragm

"How should I love a man?"

Z

I tried to love I
Tried to help
I tried to show I
Tried to tell
Support that I gave
To help you feel brave to
Help you feel saved
Helped you dig my grave

Buried with your past life
Ignored not once but
Just twice
Our conversations were
So nice
Now,

We've turned into church mice
It's hitting me from all sides
Painful like knees on dry rice
Death in this love was my price
To stay,
In love,
With a Christ

Connections are wonderful and can be made with anyone
There are a select few that have embedded themselves in me
Like vines on a vineyard wall
The fruits I've produced with these people are organic and
Always ripening
Maturing
Tending to each wall,
Each fruit,
With specialty

Tailor made regimens to suit the needs of each grape
Those who drink their wine before
It's time to harvest their produce can only enjoy it so much

Let the vines intertwine and overtake your wall;
Have enough grapes to last you through the years

Pension your grapes and
Ration wine wisely
If both tend to the garden,
You'll grow together
Intertwined you'll stay and marry one day
Drunk off of your love that
Will never
Decay

VINEYARD WALLS

V

I found myself seeing colors I never saw; viewing flowers I never thought grew; smelling fragrances to which my nose was

a stranger

There's a song that many hear,
Without words to grace the notes
The music is so deep and low,
Like a noise that rests inside the throat
Many have searched far and wide
Some conclude it can't be found
Men have climbed the tallest mountains
Even dug so deep underground

Through all the trees and blades of grass,
The hum remains a mystery
Some have found its origin
On ocean floors below the sea
To depths they dive
Fathoms below
Until they see
The Orange glow
The hum resides,
Unseen by eyes,
Of most who try,
But they'll never know

It cost too much to claim the gem that
Resonates with such passion
Men talk a lot,
And twist the plot,
With much to say,
But no action

So ill-prepared to meet the need—
Like on the breast boys come to feed and
In the end they plant their seed,
And leave

PHREKWENSEA

MAY 11, 2016

There is a sting of skepticism that fills my brain
   And a language of love that slips my tongue
I can't find the medium to blend to two
   But I know between them the war will be won
Fear and doubt may cloud the mind
While feelings of longing are left behind
With beauty and grace,
I trace your face,
With the thought of one day holding it

Within my grasp,
I hold gentle jabs of
Sweet nothings to fill your belly
I call on time to hurry with this rhyme;
To stop suspense and worry
I believe in us and you;
I believe in our bliss
Together we believe in each other;
We were always meant for this

MAY 28, 2016

I can't wait to show you my face

I can't wait to be in your space

I can't wait to breathe you in

I can't wait, my patience is thin

I can't wait to touch your skin

I can't wait to stroke your chin

I can't wait to bleed our auras

I can't wait to make new colors

I can't wait to lay on you
Chest hairs braid and lips infuse

I can't wait to hold your hand

I can't wait to make my stand
To understand that I'm your man

I can't wait to start our plan

I can't wait to see your face
I can't wait 'til you're in my space
I can't wait for this vacation

I can't wait for our confirmation

JUNE 1, 2016

Sultry and sandwiched between clouds,
I make my way to kill my doubt
Until this point you've been a dream while
Sleeping in the soundest slumber
I wait and watch the change in numbers
As time moves and feelings arrange

There's beauty in the surprise
To see that you're real
When I finally look in your eyes,
I can't imagine how good that'll feel
We'll be free from the clutch of hope,
Soaring into a new reality
One where you and I are
No longer asleep
We've found the rip in the celestial fabric:
The death of maya begins with one
Soaring the skies with heartbeats of magick
I jet through the air like rays of the sun

JUNE 2, 2016

A flick
To test the water
A slap
Just to check
A brush
To share contact
A nudge
To feel your pressure
A tug
To hold my hand
A stare
To check reality
A smile
On your face

[Embrace]

I graze my hand on your face
Kiss your cheek to
Keep things meek as
Your hands wrap with the curve of my back
I'm sure your loins have already leaked
Stolen kisses,
        Hands are held,
                Thumb brushed knuckles receive secrets
                to tell
                        Is this the start?
                        Is this the moment?
                I'm still wiping sleep from my eyes;
                        I have awoken

Confirmed

Within these few hours,
There's so much that I've learned;
There's so much to learn
The passion in me burns
With every press against your lips
When my hands are on your hips
The tingle in my fingertips:
                              God

JUNE 17, 2016

Should I weep early?
      The songs tell me so
I've started seeing the end;
      I see how you'll go

You can't take the weight,
My frail body bears just fine

You'll say you can't deal,
As I let go and cry

As you wave goodbye,
You'll ask for friendship
Don't ask me for that
It's too soon to give
I'll need time to piece back,
What you dropped and forgive

           But forgive who?
           Myself or you?
You'll break my heart in two,
          Then hand me the glue
          But where's my fault?
          I opened the vault
          I reached inside,
And gave you all and all
          I'll blame myself,
          For what you've done
I gave you the bullets,
You'll shoot with your gun
          You'll do no wrong,
          I heard the songs
You do what I saw you to do,

All along

I was told in a song
Maybe it was two
I was told to be prepared
When the leaves change,
So'll you
I'll be sure by then,
To have my own glue
'Cause all you'll do is
Hand me what's left from
What the last man gave you

JUNE 18, 2016

How am I supposed to feel,
When you tell me this isn't real?

How am I supposed to love,
When you tell me this ain't what I dreamed of?

How am I supposed to react,
When you tell me love isn't matter of fact?

So I should ride this out and
See if my face will still get smacked?

How am I supposed to be careful,
When you tell me we'll stay superficial?

You ask me what's the matter,
'Cause I worry when and where I'll shatter

"Don't think about it"
        He says
"Don't worry about it"
        He says
"That might not be true"
        He says
"But just in case, I got glue"

...he says

JUNE 18, 2016

I feel my glue has just dried and
Already,
Again,
I gave my heart to another

Did I really think this man would care with tender, fragile
hands?

I thought he wouldn't mind the jagged edges where
The breaks weren't all that clean

I try not to give my prize only to have it encased
In cycles of thorns
I don't want the man I love to bleed himself for me
A man called to embrace my muscle
He'll hug the spokes to make me feel,
That all that time,
His love was real

JULY 27, 2016

Here I come, Here I come

How dare I say no

Here I come, here I come

You gave the green light and said go

Here I come, here I come

How far will this be?

Here I come, here I come

This gesture has a fee

Here I come, here I come

You steal me away

Here I come, here I come

When'd I get this gay?

Here I come, here I come

The train is almost there

Here I come, here I come

Thank god this has air

Here I come, here I come

Express just for you

Here I come, here I come

To tell you the truth

Here I come, here I come

Eyes on your face again

Here I come, here I come

Fuck; please pass the gin

Here I come, here I come

So far from my home

Here I come, here I come

I couldn't say this on the phone

Here I come, here I come

Beat and pant in my seat

Here I come, here I come

At 59th street

Here I come, here I come

To Times Square I return

Here I come, here I come

This is going to burn

Here I come, here I come

I'm on the C

Here I come, here I come

We'll see what's meant to be

Here I am, here I am

You're at the top of the stairs

Here I am, here I am

Your hug stole all my air

Here we are, here we are

At the place where we felt sparks

Here we are, here we are

JULY 28, 2016

Grey is the day,
Like all the words we say
Working out this blend and
It seems opaque
I'm rooting for the chance,
To resolve past dilemmas
But you've done your deeds—
And "I love you" feels like a sneeze
Feeling good as it leaves,
So glad it came out but
Left wondering why,
That sneeze came about

Are we just friends?
       Are we not lovers?
             Can we still have romance,
             While seeking company in others?
You see visions of you and I and
Keep secrets behind your eyes
You wrap your arms around my waist,
And tell me that we'll be just fine

But now and again,
I say we're just friends,
Get melancholy and
Start over again
I cycle through this dark grey phase
Only to end up alone and okay
Until I bring you back to me,
Your smiles and kisses make me see that
You're the one to have and hold,
While with other men,
Seeing their love unfold

So with that notion I'll use my motion,
To keep me with me—
That includes my emotions

JULY 29, 2016

Honey to suckle while dirty fingers play in old wounds
Flavors to try while he continues to rip my hide
A pillow to bite while he fucks me raw
A muzzle to muffle as he whips with great might

Distractions they are from pain and woe
Mats to wipe my feet at the door
Tickles to swipe my skin as its smacked
Lovers to have as I make me his whore

Dreams to have as I lie on nail beds
Hearts to steal 'cause mine's between his teeth
Butterflies to catch when I kill the ones inside my belly
A fresh coat on top while layers crack underneath

RomComs to watch while I'm in a horror film
Heaven to have as I build the hell I'm in
Minds to probe when mine is scooped from my skull
Water to drink 'cause all he serves is gin

JULY 29, 2016

Seething thoughts from a cool headed boy
These thoughts so hot drive emotions to employ
A rich coat of armor that looks like a toy to
Keep myself covered when it's the pain I enjoy

Blooming so fierce my flesh from my cuts
The knife that you use tears out all my guts
And just right before those cuts try to shut
You scratch off my scabs to show me what's what

The smile that you give makes pain melt away
My small inner child may come out to play
With three small words you blurt out and say
While in my warm mouth words rot and decay

I blame you no faults as we dance this weird waltz
Our kisses are insults
The drive is all impulse
Crazed in a daze from all my mistakes
I'll make them again; why would I deviate?

AUGUST 5, 2016

He who sleeps on me awakes other suitors
The snore you belt calls attention where you lay
Until a man with another plan sees the treasure
You'll wake up and see your biggest mistake
Bloom and doom while you sit in your room
With your angst,
It consumes
While you're with your new boo
Fools times two
While he may love you,
I'll show up in spurts,
Like a game of peek-a-boo
Paths of forks make love lives cut short
Until we both finally see that you were meant for me
Or is this all desire...

Maybe?

We'll both find men who'll love us 'til the end
They'll serve as Band-Aids,
Though we're the other's medicine

He's not me and you're not him
The man who picked up the rare orange gem
But who knows the truth?
Not I nor you
We both have to see,
What's truly meant to be

SEPTEMBER 7, 2016

Infect me with visions
Sicken me with hope
Lie to me, lie to me
Give me dirt for soap
Connect with my spirit
Make me speak my truths
Climb up my fort and
Take all my jewels
Let me believe,
You can give me love
Clasp me with chains but
Let me think I'm a dove

JANUARY 10, 2017

"Time Moves Slow", BadBadNotGood

Should I say it or naw?
      Should I text it or call?
Should I tell you what's real?
      Do I tell you how I feel?
      Cause I know the deal

Shut up—
Keep it sealed

It ain't the time or place
This talk is face to face
Feelings gone but not erased
Inappropriate for this time and space

I can't deal with who you are
I won't budge nor
Survive the fall
      Is this what we've come to be?
        Secret strangers,
          Perceived enemies?
My "once upon a time"
Your "this one guy"
My dream within a dream
Your vacation from high rise steeds?

Time moves slow when
You said you had to go
I said I understood but
I don't think I ever could
I guess this is what's best:
You over there and

Me with an open chest
Emotional pneumonia;
Marijuana and bed rest
Black coffee to keep the pace
Jazz notes to pave the way

When blue moons rise in June,
That's when I speak to you
I savor the flavor,
Feelings shift my behavior
When we're done with our time,
I see I'm left behind
I keep losing the pace;
I'm losing this damn race

"Running away is easy,
        It's the leaving that's hard
Loving you was easy,
        It was your leaving that scarred"

APRIL 11, 2018

Unique frequencies in space-time between us
    How many times can this space-time relieve us?
Under deep waters I take time to feel us
    Drowning in morrows we've got time and
    freedom
Listening to waves crash on our old days
    How many ways can we recreate the phase?
    How, when, and why do we make ourselves
    crazed?
    In which dimension can we find our day?

        Twining stray colors unseen by mere mortals
          Each time I see you unlocks new portals
        Through these dark holes hides rich, new soils
        Each seed he plants sprouts fragrant, new florals

Space flowers find homes in the hollows of my heart
Glued in with love to keep the roots stable
Tell me again how you and I'll never part
I'll tell you again that you'll have to make me able

I bleed to give life to the work I create
I cry for the chance that I might participate in
Making these feelings turn into things
Giving deadweight a new pair of wings
To rid myself from
All of this hurt
And let my fresh tears
Quench the freshly turned dirt
To grow back the parts you keep in your hands with
Home grown heart parts to attract a better man

I understand that
There is a plan
I'm crucified for the sake of others,
That they might be saved from sin
I bear all the wants and feels of them all
My work is a mirror that calls all to halt
I'll take your sin and make you see
'Cause all you could ever do,
I've done shamelessly

THE ARTISTS' BURDEN

IV

VI

My mind was mine and to have that kind of control was sublime

Mourning my men

For the tenth time again

When will this end?

'Til when I say when

Love for lost boys

Lust for lost souls

Take off your clothes—

I know where this goes

I am the mirror:

You in me you see

Everything you're not

Everything you're supposed to be

For me

THRIFT SHOP DICK

JUNE 5, 2017

Strike the match and spark the flame
See the embers flick and slither
I won't know when to let it go
It makes more sense why I burn my
fingers

I see signs of a possible bloom and
Have flashed signs of heart wrenching doom
Magick fills my head when I see you,
Fear weighs my body with the feelings I have too

Why's it hard to enjoy the ride?
Behind this smile and
Brown, bright eyes
I stand ready;
Set to demonize
Already rebuking
These potential lies

Scare myself silly and
Fuck up my chances
From five minute kisses to
Side-eyed glances
'Til the man I see can
Tell me what he wants,
I'll keep myself all to myself,
Inside my little box

July 1, 2017

Indeed there's a need for you in my artistry
The question then becomes:
     Is it real or fantasy?
My heavy side thinks,
That's all up to you
Though quiet as it's kept,
     I am to blame too

We've meshed well together,
Though it hasn't been long
In this short time,
You've made my heart
Beat your song
This pump bumps to beats that
You sing with long looks
Some would say they've seen our story,
Published in a book somewhere

JULY 15, 2017

Fear is infectious
Courage is the cure
    Be that as it may,
    You're still unsure
Courage you lack;
It's courage I have
    Take latch and feed—
    I want you that bad
Our bodies braided
Purposeful indeed
    Please don't be afraid;
    I have all you need

        You said to me,

   "Let's fall in love"

        Those four words,
      Said I'm what you want

Don't fight the feeling
Give into the wave
    I promise you now,
    I won't misbehave
All of my love,
For you I will save
    All that I ask:
    With me,
        Be brave

JULY 17, 2017

Leave him alone;
He sleeps so well
    Listen to him breathe;
    Watch his lungs swell
Don't wake him up
He wants to rest
Into the sheets
He buries his chest

In his own head he wants to wander;
In his own bed he hears the call
Words that I've said,
He hears no longer
When his head hits the pillow,
    Baby,
That's all

Watch his eyes squint and
Watch his yawn lengthen
Feel his grip loosen—
His muscles are aching

    Leave him alone
    I know it's real early
    You've done this before and
    Handled it fairly
    Some things repeat,
    You're drawn to those traits
    Some things your men
    Will do all the same

Clear out your feels and
Look at what's real

Your man wants to sleep
It's not cute to steal

    Calmly retreat
    This isn't defeat
    Fall back with grace
    Just look at his face

Why get so mad
All that energy you waste—
If you stay pissed
The good parts you'll miss
He makes you smile
He tries so hard
This man makes you happy and
That's a job

       Let him sleep

AUGUST 15, 2017

Soft violence on your tongue
Flicks darkness around me
A place where we both know,
I could never feel free
A prison type space,
This jail cell I'm in:
A room with no windows
Unsure of what's happening

I'm left here to judge
          Alone here to conjure
                    By myself to interpret
                              In solitude to wonder

Do you need space or
          Are you cleaning out my space?
When will you tell me to my face?
          All this time gone to waste

                              I'm not sure what to do here

To unpack all the narratives I've been carrying for years
Tears
Caused by words of those who claimed to know me
These stories
That people created that wear my name
Don't belong to me
I've carried these versions on my back
It's time to give them back
To do away with ideas that lack the true essence,
Of me
There's nothing to grieve about
I'm my own now:
Reclaimed
Reimagined and reframed in my own light
Inspired by words of those who reflect my truest figure
Whose beauty lingers—
The flowers in my meadow who
Don't play Geppetto;
They speak of a real boy
Never coy in their depictions of me
They've tried for years to set me free from
The thoughts of monsters
From
Opinions of imposters
From lies warped by their pain
Of limited space in their brains

I am so
Cosmic

Where,
Emotion meets logic
I am,
That I am

I have all I need to make my story speak the truth

These old mes aren't mine to keep
I've lost enough sleep trying to keep up with all these
characters I play
Loyal to these lines to say to
Describe me in ways I can't relate

I've been sheltered in a room with sweltering heat that
Makes me believe that these puppets are me
I've been deceived and
Blindly received definitions from
False wordplay of what it means to be me

Today I cease

I take back the power to say who I am
Because I am,

Mine.

RECLAMATION

VII

VII

Just as quickly as my realization turned into an apology, an apology turned into a celebration.

Spirit forgives quickly.

There are no grudges in heaven— only patience and glory.

Liberate yourself and feel the unfurl
Be in the experience
Do that shit, girl
Feel that sweet spot
Rub life's clit
Strut down the avenue

25 is lit

This growth is healthy
Clothed in what fits
Feeling so wealthy
Hell no I won't quit
Freak flag is waving
This art I'm making
No one is taking
Finally no faking

Self-induced orgasms
Jack off my talents
I give myself chills
Me siento so thrilled
I look in the mirror
My vision is clearer
That head game ain't playin'
My thoughts give me shivers

I love myself
And mySelf loves me
I have enough
No need for a we
Feeling myself
Feeling on me
I love my touch
Fulfills every need
Roll up my sleeves and

Smoke my weed
Recycle my energy
Give it all to me

25

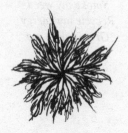

I love mySelf. I celebrate mySelf. I want mySelf to thrive. I want mySelf to be safe.

I've learned that the love I gave so freely to others is love that I deserve from myself. I'm learning that love does not mean giving the most intimate parts of myself in a hurry; a rose has thorns for a reason and the reason is void of contempt.

The love that I have for everyone is spread far and wide. Even the rays of the sun are felt more intensely the closer one gets to it.

Why else would love feel so much stronger in the embrace of another?

My love is free. My love is mine and is first and foremost for me before my cup can run over so freely.

All the things he's said to me
All the times he made me laugh
All the times he held my hand
All the times he made me mad

Every time he kissed my cheek
Every time he caught me looking
Every time he'd try to peek
All the times I'm left home cooking

Flowers he planted within my bosom
Flowers he gave to make my day
Flowers he picked to tell me he's sorry
Cause those were two words he just couldn't say

I keep them in bundles
I keep them mounds
I keep them so I can calm my heart down
I save them for me
'Cause flowers won't leave
They're left in his place
They replace his face
He left me no note
No phone call or warning
I woke up alone
To a fragrentless morning

I still smell his absence
I still feel his void
So I saved his flowers
To stop silent noise

Each one has a memory
Each one has tells a story
They all paint a history
Until that stale morning

Flowers He Gave Me

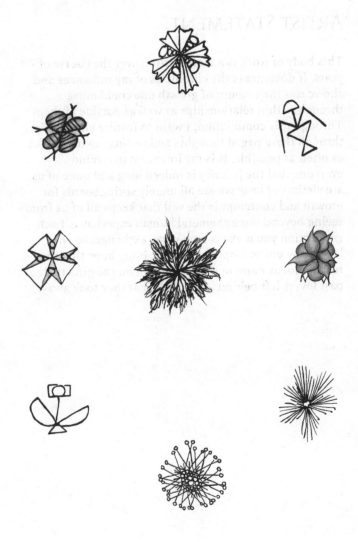

ARTIST STATEMENT

This body of work is a diary written over the course of 7 years. It documents the chronicles of my romances and showcases the amount of growth one could move through within relationships as well as outside of them. Through this compilation, I want to inspire all that flip through these paged thoughts and feelings to introspect as often as possible. It is my intention to remind everyone that the journey is indeed long and none of us are victims of love: we are all merely springboards for growth and contempt is the veil that keeps all of us from seeing beyond our ephemeral human experience. Each connection you make is a two-way exchange: *no one* leaves any union empty handed. It is my hope that the readers focus more of their attention on the gifts their past lovers left behind instead of what they took away.

About CharlesB.

CharlesB. is a poet, educator, and philosopher from Pontiac, Michigan. As an adolescent, they began writing as a way to cope with the realities of being Black and Queer in a place where the intersection of those identities seemed to define taboo itself. Encouraged heavily by James Baldwin and. E.A. Poe, their poetry and storytelling inspired CharlesB. to find and create space for their moody, introspective voice in the midst of a world that sought to silences them. CharlesB. now resides in New York City where they continue to write and work with children— validating and empowering their desire to tell their own stories and say who they are; encouraging them to access and take part in their own narratives, no matter their age, race, gender, or sexuality.

Endless Thanks

Editors
Amber S. Harrison, MA, MAPH, MLIS
Charlene Jean
Ben-Ra Wright, BS, CPT
Dan Strauss

Photography
Alex Webster

Graphic Design
Mary Olivia

Acknowledgements
My phenomenal mother, Cheryl D. Harrison
&
Daniele C. Owens, MS for her unwavering support

To everyone who has supported me throughout this
journey— Thank you

CONTENTS

As God Knits My Quilt

Δ

I| pg. 5

Δ

Men

Δ

July 13, 2011
August 3, 2011
August 5, 2011
August 9, 2011
October 26, 2011
May 3, 2012
October 13, 2013

Δ

Cliché

Δ

II| pg. 23

Δ

Where Am I?

Δ

June 28, 2012
July 28, 2012
September 2, 2012
September 8, 2012
September 26, 2012
August 15, 2014

September 30, 2016
April 4, 2017
June 29, 2017
April 22, 2018

Δ

Vineyard Walls

Δ

V | pg. 87

Δ

Phrekwensea

Δ

May 11, 2016
May 26, 2016
June 1, 2016
June 2, 2016
June 17, 2016
June 18, 2016
June 18, 2016
July 27, 2016
July 28, 2016
July 29, 2016
July 29, 2016
August 5, 2016
September 7, 2016
July 10, 2017
April 11, 2018

Δ

The Artists' Burden

Δ

Field of Flowers Playlist
Exclusively on Spotify

Follow CharlesB. on social
media:

Instagram | Twitter | Facebook

@poemsbycharles

CPSIA information can be obtained
at www.ICGtesting.com
Printed in the USA
LVHW031905070621
689603LV00008B/15

9 781737 069805